Passion Hence Forth

By Steven Helmicki

ISBN 978-0-557-30852-1

Thank you God
For the enlightenment
Real strength is Christ
Not toughness but
Kindness from the heart
Compassion
Resides in all of us
Forgiveness is

Condemnation come undone
We reside together in tranquility
Floating on the melt of
Fatty tissue advice to all
Own the past
Then let it go
Just an ancestor
To where you
Are today
And every today
Make love.

You must stop
Reliving the past
Disappeared from
Everywhere but your
Mind has moved on
Thoughts of the unconscious
Is not separate
From reality
But a cancerous
Source of excuses
Be gone
From everyone
Including me.

The road is easier
If we make it so
Appealing to be
Alive and moving
Away from the traps
Of yesterday
Calmly shifts back
To knowing ourselves
The way we were born
Pure motion.

Tell me how much
You love me
Some ask for
Quantification and stretched
Phrases of imagination
But the recipient must
Define what the giver
Of love accomplishes
With actions
We take life's gifts
With thoughts and words
We become a hostage to can't.
No more time for feeling
Extend your hands already
You can feel more than
Words.

Ancestry can be
Created today with
Relationships that thrive
Independence is not isolation
From the ones you love
Determine this warmth
Give it to everyone
Carries each other
In his world work means
Together.

It is in this place
Unity begins
To take hold of individuals
And break them down fundamentally
Through self exploration
Conclusions are drawn
Excellence for everyone
Who comes our way
We are Primordial brothers and sisters
Courageously working each day
With the light of God
Staying warm even on our coldest day
Allies for the truth
Standing together
Our song
Is the kind of strength and compassion
That guides you to a better place
All life long
Knowing Primordial
Has your back.

In a space untidy
All that was ever wrong
Represented in a few piles
Cover the good with
Too little bad
To discount life
Should be no such thing
Quit blaming yourself
For everything
But today
Is the day
You even fall asleep
With passion
Eliminating the piles
In a pleasant fire
They burn away remorse
Settling to move on
Deliberately..

The days of pink stop signs
In an altoid box
Exists with evaporated water and strength
From back in the day
Men never think
Consequences
Of anger that could have
Been forgiven
Let go
Ever so long ago
We tripped on sidewalk cracks
And shots
Always a handful to get back
On track was laid out in front
Of us we loved the rush
Too shallow to care.

The past let go
Except for review
To pick the forgotten good parts
Out of the topping
Like picking pepperoni from
The trap of cheese
That follows the mess
A slice of pie
Can be filled thinner
But much more delicious.

The antidote to all this
May be Dr. Pepper and sunshine
Stop the pace
Stillness of breath
Restoration to boy scouts
Honor a troop
Marching peacefully and free
Kid responsibility
That somehow was left
In tents and church halls
Cabins and merit badges
The streets so much less tame
Than the woods.

Battle for dominance
Pledge to toughness
For no reason at all
God's joke is one we
Play on ourselves
Hiding from Him
And then calling
For help.

A peaceful ending
Like giraffes eating together
From the same tree
The dominant and subordinate
Must eat alike
In the peace of
Atmosphere above
The lingering violence
Of ground level survival.

Can you take a dive
Back into the depths of your life
Holding your breath past
Danger points and surfacing
With life's wonders rescued
From the current confusion
Even in shifting water
Safe spaces protect
Until the sun
Glares back the angst
And warms like
A mother's hug.

Into myself I draw
A saved soul
And restart this life
On another path
To golden fields and perfect silence
Where it is impossible
To not hear
The good surrounds you
Only if you are willing
To see each other
For what they do right
Take this moment
To dare yourself
Back from the ledge of darkness
Betraying your weakness
With the Lord's strength.

The wind invades my sweatshirt
Collar is vulnerable to
Spine chilling memories
Of days gone by shaking
From fear no more
Prolonging accepting His hand
Without terms
Or caveats
I face what's in front of me
Without the vulnerability
Of days passed with its pain
Kept intact in the moment.
I carry on free
From old sin and anxiety.

Life folded me seven times
Too thick to bear
128 times the pain's
Original size is returned
unfolded like a blank page
a little wrinkled
but ironed out kinks
starting over with one word
God.

Exploding in the dampness of home
Disposing of old conflicts
Thrust out of breath
Imagining just moving in
Earning a spot to park
Despite the tight fit
Squeezing is pleasure
After licking the prize
Church bells ring
In the silence
Of box springs urges
One to the upstairs
Bend where discreet
Pleasure sleeps.

Get inside the moment
Cast upon you
In traffic a meteorite storm
Of emotions
No super hero cape
Just raw unprotected penance
Close your eyes in danger
And awaken saved
From the shield of violence
Peace protects everyone
From themselves is reborn
With God and no one
Else can claim
The Savior's
Power is yours
To absorb.

Colonize your potential
With belief
Thirst is relieved
In an astounding manner
Hunger pains leave
On the same boat with greed
When we awaken wherever
To only the good
Around us
Is stronger than hate
But harder to join
For some inherit
The bitter and save it like
Privilege in a depression
On our confidence we must rely
That being compassionate
Is the only answer
To every question.

Looking out of myself
Seeing for the first time
Like I was blind
From ambition
And driven by distrust
We sentence ourselves
To a lifetime of fault
Guilty for eating
What we like most
Ourselves are only
Everyone's equal
And nothing more.

Inside out I can turn
The waste on its side
Moving uphill
It flows down and I climb up
The central pool so distant
It hardly seems
It could have ever originated
With thoughts and actions
That are so different
From how it is
When you always
Look up to every point
That is higher than blue.

In the eyes of glass
SONY flat 7:51
The sounds off
Envisioning old shows
Daydreaming words
And lines
Today the soul must
Reduce itself to the inhuman
Knowledge that without consequence
The world may destroy itself
Trying to push aside God
With bribes in a collection basket
Salvation can never
Be found.

Imaging faulty visions
Of outgrowing reality
In the pockets lint mixed with change
More or less
Depending on how deep
You go into yourself
Despite what you save and jingle
Your eyes may tell
You are broke
From allegiance
To the only way
Home.

Crusader or Marauder what is it
That you tell
Death right before meeting
On some unforeseen corner
The bright light and laughter
Dimmed and silenced by time
Only faith can make
This place truly safe.

Born on date 3/8
It all looks so clear
From here there remains
Only one straight path
For humanity must
Be baptized in responsibility
A primordial dream
Frees the shackled
From their own dungeons
And feeds the lion of spirituality
The roar awakens
The pride to passion
The truth leads us
The top of the hill
Is quiet with rest.
Light years away
From old chaos.

The lines in my hand
History in bent knuckles
And chipped bones
Playing in the fan blades of street Darwin
Saying ouch now
Not from physical pain
But sorrow that
Redemption comes long and hard
For those taken hostage
By the hedonist villain
Known as lust.

The emperor's dream
Is forever unfulfilled
The kingdom is not
Even here
For wisdom tells
That sand and dust this becomes
An ancestor's glory
Revising untruths
That somehow a man
Conquered anything at all
Except his own necessary redemption
Must come from laying down
Arms unfolded lead to embraces
And truces
Heaven knows during war
Those fighting long
For peace.

www.ingramcontent.com/pod-product-compliance
Ingram Content Group UK Ltd.
Pitfield, Milton Keynes, MK11 3LW, UK
UKHW041901190726
13854UKWH00003B/1019

9 780557 308521